What Is Ignatian Spirituality?

WHAT IS IGNATIAN SPIRITUALITY?
DAVID L. FLEMING, SJ

LOYOLA PRESS.
A JESUIT MINISTRY
Chicago

LOYOLAPRESS.
A JESUIT MINISTRY

3441 N. Ashland Avenue
Chicago, Illinois 60657
(800) 621-1008
www.loyolapress.com

Excerpts from the *Spiritual Exercises* are from *Draw Me into Your Friendship* by David L. Fleming, SJ, published by Institute of Jesuit Sources, St. Louis, Mo., 1996.

Scripture texts in this work are taken from the *New American Bible with Revised New Testament and Revised Psalms* © 1991, 1986, 1970 Confraternity of Christian Doctrine, Washington, D.C. and are used by permission of the copyright owner. All Rights Reserved. No part of the *New American Bible* may be reproduced in any form without permission in writing from the copyright owner.

Cover design by Rick Franklin
Interior design by Maggie Hong
Cover photograph Getty Images

Library of Congress Cataloging-in-Publication Data

Fleming, David L., 1934-
   What is Ignatian spirituality? / David L. Fleming.
       p. cm
   "Excerpts from the Spiritual exercises are from Draw me into your friendship by David L. Fleming, published by Institute of Jesuit Sources, St. Louis, MO., 1996"—T.p. verso.
   ISBN-13: 978-0-8294-2718-9
   ISBN-10: 0-8294-2718-X
   1. Ignatius, of Loyola, Saint, 1491-1556. Exercitia spiritualia. 2. Spiritual life—Catholic Church. I. Title.
   BX2179.L8F575 2008
   248.3—dc22

                                                    2008023687

Printed in the United States of America
11 12 Versa 10 9 8 7 6 5 4

CONTENTS

PREFACE

Jesuits and others involved in Ignatian endeavors often refer to "our way of proceeding." This is a hard-to-define collection of attitudes, customs, and values that gives Ignatian work its characteristic flavor. Ignatius Loyola, the founder of the Jesuits, paid much attention to "our way of proceeding" when he wrote the foundational documents of the Society of Jesus. He was more interested in a whole-person approach than in rules. He did not spell out the Jesuit way of life in detail, but rather prized a certain way of thinking, praying, and behaving.

I take a similar approach in this little book. I try to answer the question "What is Ignatian spirituality?" not by systematic analysis but by describing the ideas and attitudes that make this spirituality distinctive. Ignatian spirituality is not captured in a rule or set of practices or a certain method of praying or devotional observances. It is a spiritual "way of proceeding" that offers a vision of life, an understanding of God, a reflective approach to living, a contemplative form of praying, a reverential attitude to our world, and an expectation of finding God daily. I try to capture the tone of this spirituality in a number of short essays. They are suggestive rather than exhaustive. Books can (and have been) written on all of these themes. I am trying only to describe something of the spirit of Ignatian spirituality.

For four decades I have been speaking and writing about Ignatian spirituality, directing Ignatian retreats, and training others in the art of Ignatian spiritual direction. I have found that the best way to plumb the depths of Ignatian spirituality is to reflect on Ignatius's life as he relates it in his autobiography and to draw upon the retreat experiences that find their dynamism from his classic text the *Spiritual Exercises.* I make frequent reference to the life of Ignatius Loyola and refer often to his book because, nearly five centuries after Ignatius's death, this is still the best way to grasp his innovative ideas.

I am writing for people who are drawn to Ignatian spirituality. They are people who are curious, who want to know what makes Ignatian ministries tick, who know a bit about Ignatian spirituality and want to know more, or who think they might want to learn how to pray this way. I hope these reflections will encourage readers to go deeper. Ignatius Loyola believed that God is always inviting us to respond to his presence and love. I hope that this book will show the way to a more generous response.

David L. Fleming, SJ

ACKNOWLEDGMENTS

Every author knows that the book which is published is the work of many minds and hands. Among the many people at Loyola Press who have been involved in this publication, I want to express a special thanks to Jim Manney. He labored hard to make this book a possibility, and I am deeply indebted to his gentle prodding and careful editing. I must also express my gratitude to Joe Durepos who continues to encourage me to think Ignatian thoughts and to share them in writing.

A Vision of Life, Work, and Love

In the Spiritual Exercises, Ignatius Loyola presents us with a vision in three interrelated exercises: the Principle and Foundation, the Call of the King, and the Contemplation on the Love of God. His vision takes in how we see our world, how we see our life, and how we are to grow in our relationship with God. We begin with this vision.

It's often said, "I'll believe it when I see it." But Ignatius Loyola reverses the saying: "When I believe it, I'll see it." He observed that our vision largely controls our perception. If we think the world is a bleak place, full of evil, greedy, selfish people who have no love for God or each other, that's what we will see when we look around. If we think that our world is full of goodness and opportunity, a place that God created and sustains and loves, that is what we'll find. Ignatius thought that the right vision lies at the heart of our relationship with God.

1

Ignatian spirituality offers us a vision. It is a vision of life, of work, and of love—a three-part vision that helps us see what is really true about God and about the world he created.

The Ignatian vision is contained in the *Spiritual Exercises*, the book that Ignatius Loyola assembled to help people come into a more intimate relationship with God. Ignatian spirituality flows from the Spiritual Exercises. The essence of the Ignatian vision is contained in a reflection at the beginning of the Exercises called the Principle and Foundation.

God who loves us creates us and wants to share life with us forever. Our love response takes shape in our praise and honor and service of the God of our life.

All the things in this world are also created because of God's love and they become a context of gifts, presented to us so that we can know God more easily and make a return of love more readily.

As a result, we show reverence for all the gifts of creation and collaborate with God in using them so that by being good stewards we develop as loving persons in our care of God's world and its development. But if we abuse any of these gifts of creation or, on the contrary, take them as the center of our lives, we break our relationship with God and hinder our growth as loving persons.

In everyday life, then, we must hold ourselves in balance before all created gifts insofar as we have a choice and are not bound by some responsibility. We should not fix our desires on health or sickness, wealth or poverty, success or failure, a long life or a short one. For everything has the potential of calling forth in us a more loving response to our life forever with God.

Our only desire and our one choice should be this: I want and I choose what better leads to God's deepening life in me.

Ignatius's first principle is that all creation is a gift, coming from God and leading toward God. Furthermore, "all the things in this world are . . . presented to us so that we can know God more easily and make a return of love more readily." This means that God is *in* this creation. The choices we make in our daily life in this world push us away from God or draw us closer to him. Ignatius sees God as present, not remote or detached. He is involved in the details of our life. Our daily lives in this world matter.

The Principle and Foundation is a *life vision*. It asks, "what is life all about?" It is a vision that directs us to the source of life. We will return to this life vision repeatedly in this book because it truly is the foundation of the Ignatian outlook.

Ignatian spirituality also offers a *work vision*. What is our work in this world all about? Why do we do what we do? What values should govern our choices? In the Spiritual Exercises, Ignatius asks these questions in the context of a reflection he calls the Call of the King. He proposes that we think about Jesus after the model of a king to whom we owe reverence and obedience. He is a leader with ambitious plans: "I want to overcome all diseases, all poverty, all ignorance, all oppression and slavery—in short all the evils which beset humankind," he says. He poses a challenge: "Whoever wishes to join me in this undertaking must be content with the same food, drink, clothing, and so on, that comes with following me."

Note two particular features of this work vision. Christ our king calls us to be *with* him. The essence of the call is not to do some specific work, but, above all, to be with the One who calls, imaged in the everyday details of living like our king lives. We are to share Christ's life, to think like him, to do what he does.

The second feature is a call to *work* with Christ our king. Christ is not a remote ruler commanding his forces through a hierarchy of princes, earls, dukes, lords, and knights. He is "in the trenches." He is doing the work of evangelizing and healing himself. His call goes out to every person. He wants every one to join with him, and each one receives a personal invitation. The initiative is Christ's; he asks us to work with him.

The third part of the Ignatian vision is a *vision of love*. Above all, God loves, and he invites us to love him in return. Later we will look carefully at Ignatius's Contemplation on the Love of God, which concludes the Exercises. Here we will note two statements Ignatius makes to introduce it.

The first is that "love ought to show itself in deeds over and above words." The second is that love consists in sharing: "In love, one always wants to give to the other what one has." The Spanish word that Ignatius uses here is *comunicar*—"to share or to communicate." Lovers love each other by sharing what they have, and this sharing is a form of communication. God is not just a giver of gifts, but a lover who speaks to us through his giving. God holds nothing back.

The ultimate expression of his self-giving is Jesus' death. He shares his very life with us. He also shares with us the work he is doing in the world. Thus, the work we do is a way of loving God. It is not just work. By inviting us to share in his works, God is showing his love for us. In our response of trying to work with God, we show our love.

Ignatius raises the questions: What does it mean for us to love? How do we go about expressing our love? How do we show our love for God, for ourselves, for others, and for our world? He invites us to answer these questions by looking at how God loves. He is a God who sets no limits on what he shares with us.

God Is Love Loving

In his autobiography, Ignatius describes a mystical experience of God actively involved in the creation of our world. At the beginning of the second week in the Spiritual Exercises, he imagines the Trinity coming to the decision of God-becoming-man for the salvation of our world. At the core of Ignatian spirituality is this perception of a loving God actively involved in the world.

Ignatius's life changed drastically in 1521. He was a soldier serving the kingdom of Castile, fighting to defend the city of Pamplona against a French attack. During the battle a cannonball struck him in the legs. Badly injured, Ignatius was taken to his family castle in the town of Loyola to recuperate. There he endured two extremely painful operations to repair his wounds, and spent many months convalescing. Ignatius had a lot of time to think about his life, which, to that point, had been an undistinguished and unsatisfying pursuit of military glory and frivolous pastimes.

Ignatius was a keenly observant man. His talent for simple "noticing" or "taking note" became a cornerstone of his approach to the spiritual life. In 1521, bored and restless as he healed in his family's home, Ignatius took special notice of the movements in his own spirit.

He had asked for romance novels to read. These tales of love and adventure were the most popular printed books of the time, as they are in our time, and Ignatius loved to fill his imagination with these stories. But the only books available in the house were a life of Christ and a book of stories about saints. Ignatius read these instead, and he was struck by the feelings they stirred in his heart. The stories of Jesus and the heroes of the faith inspired and stimulated him. By contrast, he was restless and discontented when he remembered his favorite tales of romantic love and adventure.

Gradually, a new and inspiring image of God began to form in Ignatius's mind. He saw God as a God of Love. This was no abstract philosophical concept. God as Love was no longer just a scriptural statement. Ignatius experienced God as an intensely personal, active, generous God, a God as Love loving. God creates, and by so doing God is actively showering us with gifts. God acts, and all his actions show his wisdom and love.

God's love is unconditional. It is not something we earn, or buy, or bargain for. God does not say, "I will love you if you keep my commandments" or "I will love you if you go to Lourdes." Lying on his sickbed—in pain, crippled, agitated—Ignatius came to understand that active loving was God's most outstanding quality. This is his foundational image of God. He arrived at it by "noting" how God dealt with him in his body, soul, and spirit, and through the people and events in his everyday life.

Ignatius saw how this image of God as an active lover profoundly affects the way we act. Because God's love is infinitely generous, we are motivated to make the most generous response we possibly can. The choices we make in life become very important. They are all about our seeking and finding the Giver of gifts. As Ignatius says in the Principle and Foundation, "All the things in this world are also created because of God's love and they become a context of gifts, presented to us so that we can know God more easily and make a return of love more readily."

This image of God affects how we understand the purpose of our lives. If we think that God loves us only if we act in a certain way, we will see our lives as a time of testing. We need to rise to the challenge, to avoid mistakes, to labor to do the right thing. But if God is Love loving, our life is a time of growing and maturing. "All the things in this world" are ways to become closer to God. Lovers don't test each other. Lovers don't constantly demand that the other measure up. Lovers give to those they love.

Our world is far from perfect. God's loved creation cries out for us to act with God to bring it to a fulfillment and so to bring about the kingdom of God, a reign of justice and love. We often abuse God's gifts by wasting them, polluting them, hoarding them, destroying them, but we can never be so pessimistic as to think that God will be defeated by our bad use of his gifts. God came into his creation in a definitive way in Jesus Christ. With the defining life, death, and resurrection of Jesus, God has entered into the assured victorious struggle against every limiting factor, whether physical, psychological, or spiritual.

Reflection on God's gifts is the first part of Ignatius's Contemplation on the Love of God, the concluding prayer of the Spiritual Exercises. Here, Ignatius has us consider all that God has given to us—our life, our family, our friends, perhaps husband or wife or religious community, our talents and education, our native country and the times in which we live, our faith, our church, the forgiveness of our sin, and the promise of life forever with God.

Then Ignatius tells us how God is not content with just giving us gifts; God gives us *himself* in Jesus, his only Son. Jesus gives himself to us in his life, passion, and death, and he continues to be present to us in his resurrected life. Jesus gifts us with himself in the Eucharist, where he literally puts himself in our hands. We become his hands and his feet and his voice in our world.

Ignatius then points to God's continuing efforts on our behalf. God is not a distant, snap-of-the-fingers, miracle-working God. Our God is a God who labors over his creation. In Jesus, God is born in an occupied country, lives the life of an itinerant preacher, is betrayed, put to death, raised up. This is a God who labors with and through his church to bring to fulfillment the redeemed creation. Ignatius sees God as a busy God, involved in a labor of love.

Ignatius ends the contemplation by stressing the limitless nature of God's love. God has broken through all barriers, even the barrier of death. Ignatius compares the gifts of God to the light that pours forth inexhaustibly from the sun. He compares them to the waters that flow from a spring-source. But even these are pale images of the mighty flow of love that gushes forth from the heart of the Lover.

This is the God whom Ignatius would have us know. He is Love loving, and we, his loved ones, can generously share with this God everything we have.

A SPIRITUALITY OF THE HEART

In the exercise the Call of the King, Ignatius says that there are two responses to God's call. One response comes from the reasonable person. The second response is from the generous or magnanimous person. We might call it the response of the heart.

Ignatius prefaced his Spiritual Exercises with twenty notes that explain the purpose of his exercises and offer advice and counsel to the director who is guiding the retreat. The very first of these "preliminary helps" explains what he means by *spiritual* exercises. Physical exercise tunes up the body and promotes good health. Spiritual exercise, he writes, is good for "strengthening and supporting us in the effort to respond ever more faithfully to the love of God."

Note what Ignatius did not say. He did not say that the Spiritual Exercises are designed primarily to deepen our understanding or to strengthen our will. He did not promise to explain spiritual mysteries to us or enlighten our minds.

We may emerge from the Exercises with enhanced intellectual understanding, but this is not the goal. The goal is a response—a certain kind of response. Ignatius is after a response of the heart.

"Heart" does not mean the emotions (though it includes our emotions). It refers to our inner orientation, the core of our being. This kind of "heart" is what Jesus was referring to when he told us to store up treasures in heaven instead of on earth, "for where your treasure is, there also will your heart be." (Matthew 6:21) This is the "heart" Jesus was worried about when he said "from the heart come evil thoughts, murder, adultery, unchastity, theft, false witness, blasphemy." (Matthew 15:19) Jesus observed that our heart can get untethered from our actions: "This people honors me with their lips, but their hearts are far from me." (Matthew 15:8) Heart in this sense—the totality of our response—is the concern of the Spiritual Exercises.

This is the ancient meaning of "heart" in biblical usage, but we actually retain traces of this meaning in contemporary English. When we say to someone "my heart goes out to you," we mean something more than a feeling of concern. If said sincerely, it communicates a sense of solidarity with someone. It means more than "I understand" (our intellect). It means more than "I sympathize" (our feelings). It means something like, "I stand with you in this." It is an expression of a fundamental choice.

Today we commonly say about someone who shows no enthusiasm for a project that "his heart isn't in it." We usually say this when people behave in a way that is at odds with their deepest desires. We say it about ourselves when we hurt people that we love and do things that we know are at odds with who we really are. This "heart" is what Ignatius is concerned with. We might think about Ignatian spirituality as a way of getting our hearts in the right place.

Ignatius understood this because that is what happened to him. He underwent a profound conversion while recuperating from his wounds, but it was not a conversion of the intellect or will. Before his conversion—and afterward—he was a thoroughly orthodox Catholic who followed the religious practices expected of him. That was not what changed. His conversion involved his deepest desires and commitments, that essential center of the personality in which man stands before God. His religious practice and intellectual understanding deepened over time, but it was his heart that was transformed.

Over years of prayerful reflection and spiritual direction of others, Ignatius developed many ways to listen to the language of the heart. This is the language that reveals God's intentions and inspires us to a generous response. What we believe and what we do are important. But Ignatius is far more interested in the condition of our hearts.

Still, most of us face a persistent temptation to make the Spiritual Exercises or any kind of spiritual renewal a matter of changing the way we think. Indeed, this danger arises even in a book like this, which sets forth ideas and concepts and principles to broaden our understanding of Ignatian spirituality. It is vital to realize that understanding is not the goal. We can understand a great number of things, but this may not affect the way we live our lives. The goal is a response of the heart, which truly changes the whole person.

God taught Ignatius about the heart through several mystical visions he received early in his spiritual formation. One such vision came upon him at a time when he was questioning whether he should say three or four prayers to our Trinitarian God—a prayer directed to each Person, Father, Son, and Spirit, and then a fourth prayer to the One God. He was praying outside on the steps of a monastery when he suddenly "heard" God the Trinity as the musical sound of three organ keys playing simultaneously. Another time he received a vision of God the creator as "something white out of which rays were coming." Out of this whiteness God created light. "He did not know how to explain these things," he writes of himself in the third person. But Ignatius responded with his heart: "This was accompanied with so much tears and so much sobbing that he could not restrain himself."

This heart response is a cornerstone of the Spiritual Exercises. Creation is a flow of God's gifts, with a human response being the link that allows the flow to return to God. The human response is a free choice to allow God's creation to speak. Creation helps us to know and love God and to want to live with God forever.

Early in the Exercises, Ignatius asks the retreatant to pray before Jesus Christ on the cross. He identifies Christ as creator, the God of the Principle and Foundation. "Talk to him about how he creates because he loves," Ignatius seems to say. This is no abstract God of reason, but a loving God seen in the face of Jesus Christ. It is the Pauline Christ of Colossians and Ephesians. It is the Christ of the Prologue to John's Gospel: the Word "in whom all things were created." This is the Son of God, the Alpha and Omega of John's Apocalypse.

Our spiritual journey is an attempt to answer the question, "What is life all about?" Here is Ignatius's answer: a vision of God for our hearts, not our minds. It is a depiction of the Creator as a superabundant giver. He gives gifts that call forth a response on our part, a free choice to return ourselves to him in grateful thanks and love. It is a vision that only a heart can respond to.

A Reflective Spirituality

In the Spiritual Exercises, the first way of praying that Ignatius introduces is a way of discerning the presence of God by reflecting on our daily experience. Ignatius's emphasis on the *examen* (his term for this way of praying) underlines the importance of personal reflection in Ignatian spirituality.

The goal of the spiritual life, as Ignatius conceived it, is to "choose what better leads to God's deepening life in me." This is a dynamic goal. We are to *choose*—to freely unite ourselves with God. Most of the time this means that we are to join with God in active work in the world.

This active life rests on a foundation of reflection. Ignatian spirituality teaches us to discern the footprints of God in our own experience. It shows us how to look back on our lives, to sift through our memories in order to see the way God has been dealing with us over the years. It teaches us how to find God in the present moment—in the relationships, challenges, frustrations, and feelings that we are experiencing today. The tools and methods of Ignatian spirituality instill in us habits of prayerful, thoughtful reflection.

Ignatius made this clear in the way he arranged the Spiritual Exercises. He begins the retreat with the Principle and Foundation, which states in concise form Ignatius's vision of God's purposes in creating ("to share life with us forever"), the purpose of the things he created ("presented to us so that we can know God more easily and make a return of love more easily"), and the goal of the retreat ("to choose what better leads to God's deepening life in me"). Ignatius then presents a method of reflective prayer that he calls "the particular and daily *examen*." This surprises many who undertake the Exercises. The *examen* seems to be a digression from the real business of the retreat.

But Ignatius deliberately put the *examen* at the beginning. The *examen* is an indispensable tool to realize the purpose of the Spiritual Exercises—to detect God's presence and to discern his will through close attention to the subtle interior movements of God's spirit. It is the cornerstone of Ignatian prayer.

Ignatius wanted his Jesuits to make the *examen* a daily habit. He understood that the press of work or illness might sometimes make it impossible for Jesuits to have an extended time of daily prayer. But he insisted that they never omit the *examen*. Twice a day, about midday and again before retiring, Jesuits were to pause for a while and review the events of the day in a spirit of prayerful reflection. This is one of the few rules Ignatius laid down for prayer.

The *examen* that Ignatius outlined in the Spiritual Exercises has five points: 1) be grateful for God's blessings; 2) ask the help of the Spirit; 3) review the day, looking for times when God has been present and times when you have left him out; 4) express sorrow for sin and ask for God's forgiving love; 5) pray for the grace to be more totally available to God who loves you so totally. Over the years, Jesuits and others have developed many versions of the *examen*. They are like successive editions of a great textbook. They are based on the same insight and ideas, but they differ in order to emphasize certain things and to adapt to diverse audiences.

Because the word *examen* seems to indicate a kind of introspection, probably the greatest emphasis should be placed on the *examen* as praying. Ignatius tries to emphasize this point by making his first point of the *examen* prayer one about gratitude to God.

We might outline the *examen* prayer as follows:

THE EXAMEN OF CONSCIOUSNESS

A Prayer to God

God, thank you.

I thank you, God, for always being with me, but
especially I am grateful that you are with me
right now.

God, send your Holy Spirit upon me.
God, let the Holy Spirit enlighten my mind and
warm my heart that I may know where and
how we have been together this day.

God, let me look at my day.
God, where have I felt your presence, seen your face,
heard your word this day?
God, where have I ignored you, run from you,
perhaps even rejected you this day?

God, let me be grateful and ask forgiveness.
God, I thank you for the times this day we have been
together and worked together.
God, I am sorry for the ways that I have offended you
by what I have done or what I did not do.

God, stay close.
God, I ask that you draw me ever closer to you this
day and tomorrow.
God, you are the God of my life—thank you.

Sometimes our prayer can get formal and abstract. The Daily Examen keeps our feet on the ground. This reflective, Spirit-led review of the day grounds our prayer in concrete reality. Because we are God's sons and daughters living in a world that he loves and sustains, we can be assured that we can hear his voice in our lives in this world.

There is one final advantage to making a habit of the Daily Examen: We will never run out of things to pray about. Sometimes prayer gets dry. Sometimes we wonder what to say to God. The *examen* eliminates these problems. As long as we have twenty-four hours to look back on, we will have hundreds of things to talk to God about—and to thank him for.

Sin Is a Lack of Gratitude

In his autobiography, Ignatius describes himself as a man at one time beset with a terrible scrupulosity about his own sinfulness. He tried many human remedies, but eventually he had to throw himself on the mercy of God. Sin, he then saw, might be better viewed through two prisms. We might see sin as a lack of gratitude in the face of God's continuing gifting. And sin can also be viewed as a lack of reverence for the One I call the God of my life.

Something is badly wrong. Our world is full of suffering and evil. We feel disorder in our own hearts. We often feel an irresistible tug to turn our backs on God. The Christian term for this disorder is *sin*. Sin is an integral part of the gospel. It is the sickness of the world that Christ came to heal, the enemy that we are called to vanquish. But what is sin? Theologians and philosophers labor to understand it. Christians often sink into a mire of guilt and introspection as they contemplate it.

Ignatius Loyola's attitude toward sin is characteristically innovative, but all of a piece with his spiritual insights. He takes sin very seriously. He wants us to confront our own sin; he even has us pray for the grace of "shame and confusion" as we consider our offenses. But these personal responses are the result of graces. They are gifts from God, like all his other gifts. Ignatius always looks at sin within the context of God's love. Sin is essentially a failure of gratitude. We sin because we do not fully grasp what God has done for us.

The entire first week of the Spiritual Exercises is given over to reflection on sin and evil in our world and in ourselves. Ignatius is not interested in having us understand sin. Sin is part of the mystery of evil and cannot be fully grasped by the mind anyway. Rather, he wants us to comprehend sin with our hearts. We are to proceed in prayer, praying for grace, asking God to reveal to us how God sees sin.

He has us look at sin first as an objective phenomenon. We look at the sin of the angels who rebelled against God. Like all created beings, they were presented with the choice to freely respond to the love that God offers. Some spirits rejected God and suffered the loss of sharing divine life as a consequence. Then we turn to Adam and Eve, parents of the human race, who chose wanting to be their own gods rather than sharing divine life. Finally Ignatius invites us to objectively consider the mortal sin of one person who definitively chooses self over God. Terrible consequences flow from a single free choice. The awfulness of sin is seen not in the count of numbers—how many sins—but in the face of a God who keeps loving us.

This appraisal of the objective reality of sin will soon lead to a consideration of our own personal sin, but first Ignatius asks us to imaginatively come into the presence of Jesus on the Cross. We are to consider what Christ did in response to sin. Then we ask ourselves three questions: What have I done for Christ? What am I doing for Christ? What ought I to do for Christ? This is the all-important context within which we view sin. The suffering and death of Jesus is God's response to sin. The "face" of sin is reflected in the suffering face of the crucified Christ. We contemplate the terrible fact of sin, and the shameful reality of our own sin, in the blinding light of God's Love, crucified on a cross. Ignatius once again raises the insistent question that resonates throughout Ignatian-influenced spirituality: How am I to respond?

Ignatius invites us to look at our own history of sin and evil in light of the goodness of God. Even though we reject God, he still blesses us. The saints and angels still pray for us. The earth does not swallow us up. Rather we enjoy the bounty of God's splendid creation—"heavens, sun, moon, stars, and elements, fruits, birds, fishes, and animals." Sin is not the breaking of a law or commandment as much as it is a lack of gratitude. It is an offense against the quality of *acatamiento*—a Spanish word meaning "reverence" that is one of Ignatius's favorite words to describe the honor due to God. We stand in awe before the majesty of God, the One who is the Giver of the whole of our life. How can we offend the God of our life? If our heart could truly grasp what God is doing for us, how could we sin? We would be too grateful to sin.

Even though we are sinners, we can respond to God's invitation to join him. This is another prominent theme of Ignatian spirituality. We sometimes feel that we have to first "clean up our act" in order to grow spiritually. But we do not have to wait. There is work to be done.

That is why Ignatius mingles sorrow for sin with resolve to follow Christ in the first week of the Exercises. The two go together. As we mature as followers of Christ, we grow in our sensitivity to sin. We become more aware of the ways in which we wrong God, and of the ways we wrong other people and they wrong us. We become more eager to seek forgiveness for ourselves and to grant forgiveness to other people. Often, people appreciate the sacrament of penance and reconciliation more after they have made some progress in the spiritual life than they did at the beginning. This is what the prodigal son felt when he returned home. The young man had repented. He had changed his life. Yet he was stricken with sorrow at his sin when he returned home. His father's compassionate love highlighted his failures and underlined his need for forgiveness. But his father embraces him in love, even stifling his practiced words of repentance.

One of the great gospel stories about sin and forgiveness is the account of Jesus' meal at the home of Simon the Pharisee. A woman known as a public sinner entered the room and tearfully anointed Jesus' feet with fine ointment. When the Pharisee objected to such close contact with a sinner, Jesus explained that the woman knew she had much to be thankful for: "her many sins have been forgiven; hence, she has shown great love." (Luke 7:47)

The woman was a prostitute. In the Old Testament prostitution is a symbol for sin. All sin is prostitution of a kind. It is a kind of love that is sold for a price, a love wrongly directed to people and things, a choice to love something that we put in place of God. When we realize our tragic failure, we become sorrowful and we eagerly seek forgiveness. The result is a closer relationship with Jesus and a renewed ability to give and to receive love, and, even better, to receive a forgiving love and to be enabled to offer forgiveness to others.

The Spiritual Life Is a Pilgrimage

In his autobiography, Ignatius refers to himself as "the pilgrim." Pilgrims are not wanderers, vagrants, or aimless travelers; pilgrims have a set destination, though the roads may be many and varied in getting to the destination. For Ignatius, the spiritual life is a true pilgrimage and requires not a map but a "way of proceeding" to get to the destination.

In his last years, Ignatius dictated a brief account of his life to a fellow Jesuit named Luis Gonzalez de Camara. He did so reluctantly, only because Camara and other close associates in the Jesuit order begged him to. Ignatius was a modest man with no interest in trumpeting his accomplishments. Nevertheless his friends knew that Ignatius's spiritual ideas were deeply rooted in the events of his life and they wanted a record of his experiences in his own words. It is a precious document that enhances our understanding of Ignatius and Ignatian spirituality in innumerable ways.

Throughout this account of his life, Ignatius refers to himself as "the pilgrim." This was true in a literal sense for a time. When he first dedicated his life to God he set out on a pilgrimage to the Holy Land. If they had the means, this was what men of his time were supposed to do when they got serious about Christianity, and Ignatius did what was expected of him. However, Ignatius looked at his entire life as a pilgrimage in a broader sense. His journey seemed for a time to be a meandering one. For many years he pursued a goal indistinctly seen by him. He wandered across a good part of Europe on foot. He explored different approaches to the spiritual life. It took time for Ignatius and his early Jesuit companions to settle on the mission for their order.

The idea of setting forth on a spiritual pilgrimage is common today in our age of "seeker" spirituality. It was not so common in Ignatius's time. For most, the spiritual life was a settled thing. It was lived in a single place, in monasteries and convents, in small towns and villages, and governed by chanting the Divine Office (the Liturgy of the Hours), pious practices, and seasonal devotions. Or it was circumscribed by an explicit mission—for example, the evangelical poverty of the Franciscan friars and the preaching and scholarship of the Dominicans. Ignatius broke with these models. He had a clear destination: "I want and I choose what better leads to God's deepening life in me," as he put it in the Principle and Foundation in the Spiritual Exercises. But the way of getting there was a winding road. Ignatius would have us identity with the Jesus who said, "Foxes have dens and birds of the sky have nests, but the Son of Man has nowhere to rest his head." (Matthew 8:20)

We might look at Ignatian spirituality as a set of basic attitudes about the pilgrimage we are on. Our response to God is not a one-time, settled thing. Circumstances will change and new opportunities will open up. God will point in new directions. We need to always stay alert and seize the opportunities we have every day. The tools of Ignatian spirituality keep us attentive to the movements of the Holy Spirit. Of special importance is the Daily Examen, a method of detecting God's presence through a prayerful review of the events of the day. Ignatian spirituality offers a broad understanding of prayer as continuous mutual sharing and intimate communication. But Ignatian spirituality also gives us techniques of imaginative prayer, which put us in touch with the living Christ of the Gospels.

The pilgrimage is all about following Jesus. Though he had a rich devotional life, Ignatius does not offer us a pot-pourri of devotional practices. He does not preach at us. He doesn't draw moral lessons from the Gospel texts. Instead he puts the person of Jesus at the center of our lives and asks us to follow him. Ignatius thought that the purpose of a pilgrimage to Jerusalem is to "kiss the spot where the gentle Jesus stood or sat or performed some deed." He would have us feel the same reverence for Jesus during our pilgrimage. We think of him in preparation for prayer. We look at him and listen to him during our prayer. To be a pilgrim is to let ourselves be led by the Lord.

Pilgrims are people on "a way." The Acts of the Apostles tells us that the earliest Christians were known as "people of the Way." They lived according to "the way of Jesus." It was a way of living their daily lives, a distinctive way that others noticed. Ignatius refined this notion of "way" when he wrote the Jesuit Constitutions, which describe the way of life of the Jesuit order. Ignatius's main idea was that Jesuits were to be available for apostolic work. He knew that their itinerant life should not be circumscribed by a lot of prescriptive rules. Instead, he outlined a "way of proceeding." This was a set of attitudes, approaches, and customs that Jesuits would internalize during their formation. The way of proceeding would offer a trustworthy guide to decisions as Jesuits lived their pilgrim journey.

The Ignatian way prizes flexibility and adaptability. It is based on an understanding that God is present in our world and is ever-eager to enlist us in his work of healing and redeeming it. It understands that God seeks to communicate with us in many ways, especially in the circumstances of our daily lives. It is a habit of consistently reflecting on our experience in order to discern God's presence in it and his direction for us. It is a method of prayer that brings us imaginatively into the life of Jesus so that we can know, love, and follow him.

These are some of the traits that make up the Ignatian way of proceeding. A way of proceeding is a key concept in Ignatian spirituality. It is an approach toward the spiritual life, not a spiritual system. It is one of the reasons why Ignatian spirituality is so congenial to so many contemporary people.

The Ignatian way of proceeding is a reliable way to live our lives as pilgrims. Equipped this way, we can be assured that we can follow Jesus in all circumstances, no matter how winding the road.

GOD CALLS, WE RESPOND

In the Call of the King exercise, Ignatius pictures the risen Christ calling every person to follow him. God takes the initiative. We respond to his call. Here we reflect on this Ignatian dynamic.

Ignatian spirituality asks the question: *What more does God want of me?* Ignatius had a profound insight into God and his creation, and he developed many prayer methods, rules for discernment, spiritual disciplines, and approaches to apostolic service. But all these elements of Ignatian spirituality are ways to help us answer a single burning question, "What more does God want now?"

God calls. We respond. It is the fundamental dynamic of the spiritual life. The concluding prayer exercise at the end of the Spiritual Exercises shows God pouring his limitless love and his gifts down on the world, "like the light rays from the sun." This is not just a global vision. God is active in each of us personally. The purpose of the Spiritual Exercises, writes Ignatius, is to facilitate the movement of God's grace within us "so that the light and love of God inflame all possible decisions and resolutions about life situations."

God is an active God. He is ever at work in people's lives, inviting, directing, guiding, proposing, suggesting. This understanding of God animates Ignatian spirituality and gives it its internal cohesion. The techniques and practices associated with Ignatian spirituality are all designed to help us be more attentive to this active God. Ignatian spirituality can be described as an active attentiveness to God joined with a prompt responsiveness to his leading.

Our response to God occurs *now*. We are not to be inhibited by our own weakness and failure. We are not to ponder our unworthiness. God is working in our lives now and we are to respond now.

This is certainly Jesus' attitude when he called the first disciples. One day on the Sea of Galilee Jesus directed Peter to cast his nets into a place on the lake where Peter had had no luck fishing. Peter objects, but makes an enormous catch, a clear sign of his call as one of Jesus' followers. He immediately raises the "unworthy" objection. "Depart from me, Lord, for I am a sinful man," he says. This is certainly true, but Jesus ignores him. "Do not be afraid; from now on you will be catching men," he says. (Luke 5:8,10)

Jesus surrounded himself with sinners. Ignatius draws our attention to the call of Matthew. He was a tax collector, an agent of the hated Romans, who made his living by extracting money from destitute peasants. Jesus encountered Matthew sitting at his customs post and said simply "Follow me." The sinner's response: "He got up and followed him." Matthew threw a party to celebrate his new life; he invited his old friends to come and meet his new ones: "many tax collectors and sinners came and sat with Jesus and his disciples." When the Pharisees objected to this spectacle Jesus replied, "I did not come to call the righteous but sinners." (Mark 2:14,15,17)

The Gospels show us Jesus entering into people's lives and inviting them to follow him—right from where they are, from boats and fishnets and from tax booths. He does not demand first that they run to the synagogue. Neither should we delay our response to God until we deal with our neuroses and character defects and our own sinful behaviors.

Our response to God grows and matures and deepens over time. It is a process, not an event. Paul writes to the Corinthians that "I fed you milk, not solid food, because you were unable to take it." (1 Corinthians 3:2) God will give us what we need. If we are beginners, or if we are troubled and weak, God will give us milk. Later on we will have solid food. All along the path we will be answering God's call to "follow me."

Our response to God has a particular quality to it. Our response is a *response.* God initiates; we answer. We do not strike out on our own. We are to "follow." To follow means that we adopt a kind of active passivity toward the action of God. "Active passivity" captures the characteristic tone of Ignatian spirituality. It is a spirituality of attentiveness, of watching and waiting, of noticing the ebb and flow of our feelings and inner dispositions. We are like the servant and maid in Psalm 123:

> Yes, like the eyes of a servant
> on the hand of his master,
> Like the eyes of a maid
> on the hand of her mistress,
> So our eyes are on the LORD our God. (Psalm 123:2)

The question we seek an answer for is "What more does God want of me?" *More* is the *magis* of Ignatian spirituality—the aspiration to always grow in service for the greater glory of God. *Magis* has been described as the Jesuit "itch"—a restlessness in service, an ambition to maintain high standards of performance, a desire to conquer new frontiers. But it simply means *more*. We are loved by a God who loves without limit. We love him in return. What more can we do to love him?

This is the question that the rich young man asked Jesus in the Gospels. "What must I do to inherit eternal life," he asked Jesus. Jesus reminded him of his duties as a good Jew: to love God, keep the commandments, and love his neighbor. "All of these I have observed from my youth," he replied. He wants to do *more*. At this, "Jesus, looking at him, loved him." He tells the young man to get rid of his possessions, and to "follow me." (Mark 10: 17–21)

Jesus challenges the young man—and us—to be free of what we claim as our own. This may be our material or worldly possessions. It may be our ideas and our desires. God calls us to be free of these things, claiming them as our own. Will we offer them to God and to God's shaping and forming and using them? He looks on us with love. What more can we do to respond to this love?

God Communicates in Many Ways

In his autobiography, Ignatius describes how he began to "notice" or "take note" of God working with him both within (through interior movements) and without (through the events of his day). "Noticing" alerted Ignatius to the many ways that God communicates with us in everyday life. Of course, he begins with Jesus, the Word of God.

Ignatius Loyola was quite possibly the most media-savvy man of the sixteenth century. He wrote letters constantly to his Jesuits, to benefactors, church officials, friends, and acquaintances—more letters than any other notable figure of his age. He insisted that Jesuits in the far-flung missions make monthly reports. He installed the first printing press in Rome. He loved the theater. He pushed his Jesuits to master the performance art of public preaching. He was a superb fundraiser and an adroit practitioner of public relations. Ignatius used all the tools at hand to say what he had to say.

He was convinced that God did the same thing, and he was only imitating God in what he did. Ignatian spirituality sees God as a "media God." God is ever-present, constantly in touch, communicating with us in many ways: in prayer and reading scripture, of course, but also through the events of our lives—through the people we meet and the work we do, through the things we see and hear, through our interior moods and affections.

God's voice is usually quiet, often indirect. He is heard, as the prophet Elijah heard him, in "a tiny whispering sound." Ignatius knew that the ears of our heart have to be trained to detect God's voice, and he developed techniques to do this.

We have to learn to listen to God's language. You have probably had the experience of conversing with people who are not native speakers of your language. Even though they may be highly educated adults who are perfectly fluent in English, we tend to slow down and raise our voice when we talk to them. Subconsciously, we treat them like children who have trouble hearing and understanding what we say.

Too often we pray this way. We do all the talking. We tell God what we want slowly and loudly. We are afraid he cannot hear us and will not understand us. Ignatius would have us stop talking so much and listen instead.

God is speaking to us in many ways in our everyday life. Ignatius makes this point at the very beginning of the Spiritual Exercises. In the Principle and Foundation, he writes that God created us out of love, and that we are to make a love response in return. Then he writes, "all the things in this world are also created because of God's love and they become a context of gifts, presented to us so that we can know God more easily and make a return of love more readily." *All the things in this world* are here *so that we can know God more easily*. We have a satellite television with 500 channels. God is broadcasting on all of them.

Most other approaches to the spiritual life concentrate on one or two of these channels. They emphasize finding God in fixed-hour prayer throughout the day, in prayerful reading of scripture, in certain devotional practices, and in fasting and other disciplines of self-denial. Many spiritualities assume that we hear God best in solitude and quiet, ideally in a place radically separated from the world. By contrast, Ignatian spirituality seeks God's voice in all the things of this world. It is the difference between a drab black-and-white silent movie and a feature film in full sound and color.

The "media event" that gives rise to this Ignatian emphasis is the Incarnation, whereby God became human in the person of Jesus Christ. The Ignatian emphasis on a media God recognizes that God is present in his creation and uses all aspects of creation to speak to us.

Incarnation is an abstract theological word. To make the Incarnation alive in our hearts, Ignatius asks us to imagine it. In the second week of the Spiritual Exercises he asks us in our prayer to place ourselves with the triune God, "looking down on our world: men and women being born and being laid to rest . . . the old and the young, the rich and the poor, the happy and the sad, so many people aimless, despairing, hateful, and killing . . . so many struggling with life and blind to any meaning. With God I can hear people laughing and crying, some shouting and screaming, some praying, others cursing." We immerse ourselves in the sights and sounds of this suffering world.

Then, Ignatius writes, "I notice how our triune God works—so simply and quietly, so patiently."

The scene shifts to Nazareth, where Mary is visited by an angel and invited to become the mother of the savior. We look at Mary, ourselves totally present in the scene, "hearing the nuances of the questions, seeing the expression in the face and eyes, watching the gestures and movements that tell us so much about a person." We, like God, wait to hear Mary's response.

Then God acts. Jesus is born of poor parents in an occupied land and knows the experience of living as a refugee. The project of salvation is set in motion. God enters into the messiness of human living, even into its most unfair, cruel, and death-dealing aspects.

God is not an absent God. The problem is that often we are too busy and too self-focused to notice him. The paramount revelation of God is Jesus. To live, St. Paul says, is "to know Christ Jesus." Jesus says to Philip, "if you have seen me you have seen the Father." Ignatius would have us carefully enter into a contemplative way of knowing Jesus in the Gospels. We become like Jesus' disciples—following him, listening to him, seeking to understand him, responding to his call.

Quiet reflection, patient noticing—this is how we hear the media God who is ever-present.

PRAYER IS A
CONVERSATION

For Ignatius, an ordinary Spanish word, *conversar*, becomes a central way of describing our relationship with God and our ministry with others. *Conversar* means "a dealing with," "an interacting with," as well as "a conversing with," or a "talking with." *Conversar* describes simply an Ignatian approach to prayer and ministry.

From the beginning of his spiritual journey, Ignatius had a good idea of what he wanted to do. He wanted to evangelize, to bring the good news of the Incarnation to others. He wanted to lead others into a relationship with Christ Jesus.

How to accomplish this was less clear. It took years for him to develop the attitudes, insights, and techniques that we know as Ignatian spirituality. He made many mistakes along the way and wandered down several blind alleys. He was familiar with the work of the Dominicans—an order of learned clerics who specialized in the ministry of preaching. Ignatius admired good preaching, but this was not the evangelistic tool he was looking for. Ignatius was attracted to the Franciscans, who gave a powerful witness to the gospel through their poverty. But he did not think that humble itinerant begging was the direction God wanted him to take.

Some spiritual approaches seemed too passive to him. They were based on reading books and listening to sermons and lectures. They appeared to say that God can be found through some kind of passive absorption of good will and good behavior. Ignatius practiced an active spirituality. He understood that people were actively engaged with work in the world. They had dealings with each other. They shared life with each other. This active sharing of grace and gifts and talents eventually became the *how* for his evangelistic ministry.

Ignatius describes his ministry by the simple Spanish word *conversar. Conversar* means "to converse," "to talk with." Its simplest meaning in English is sincere talk with another person, the kind of comfortable, satisfying conversation whereby we truly get to know someone else. Ignatius must have been a master of this kind of conversation. He seems to have had an extraordinary gift for friendship. The first Jesuits were a group of men who were initially bound together by their affection and love for Ignatius Loyola.

Conversar has broader meanings as well. It means "to be conversant with" something or someone—that is, to truly know them deeply. It means "to have dealings with." To converse with someone is to know them and to be involved with their lives. In the Ignatian scheme of things, to converse is one of our ways of loving.

Ignatius's spiritual life developed around the idea of conversation. It is based on conversation with God in prayer. It is developed through conversation with others—spiritual directors, confessors, like-minded friends who share one's ideals and way of life. It is expressed in conversation as ministry—sharing the gospel with others. All three conversations are embodied in the Spiritual Exercises. The retreatant is guided through the exercises by conversation with a spiritual director who cultivates the conversation with God. The exercises nurture a conversation with God. The goal of the Exercises is to help the person get involved in a more fruitful conversation with others in ministry.

In fact, the Exercises themselves are the product of years of conversation. Ignatius developed them from his experience as a spiritual director of men and women seeking a deeper relationship with God. He would suggest ways to pray, scripture passages to meditate on, scenes to imagine, ideas to ponder. Then he and his friends would talk about what happened in prayer. Together they would discern how God seemed to be leading. Ignatius's book, perhaps the most influential book ever written about developing our relationship with God, is essentially a collection of these exercises, sharpened and honed in conversation.

The Spiritual Exercises are structured around the developing relationship between the retreatant and Jesus Christ. They urge us to see ourselves as God sees us—as his sons and daughters, members of his family. Jesus used the affectionate word *abba* to refer to his Father when he prayed. The closest English equivalent is "Papa." We can address God in the same intimate, friendly way because we are his children.

Prayer is a natural outcome of this close relationship. It is not something mysterious or esoteric or something that we learn how to do in school. Prayer is conversation. If we can talk, we can pray. Of course we can learn to pray better, just as we can learn to be better conversationalists. That, in fact, was Ignatius's intention in putting together his Spiritual Exercises. But the essential activity of prayer springs naturally from our humanity. It is a matter of conversing with a very good friend.

Consider what Jesus did when the disciples asked him, "Lord, teach us to pray." Did these good Jewish men, who prayed five times a day (at least), really mean that they did not know how to pray? Hardly. They wanted to know Jesus' way of praying. So he taught them the Our Father, which is the template of all Christian prayer.

Jesus' way of praying is more important than the words he taught us. We are personally familiar with God ("*our* Father"). We reverence him ("who art in heaven," "hallowed be thy name"). We share God's desires ("thy kingdom come," "thy will be done"). We ask for what we need ("give us this day our daily bread"). We beg our Father's protection ("deliver us from evil").

These elements of prayer cover the whole range of human conversation: sharing experience, saying thank you, asking for help, crying out in pain, begging forgiveness, expressing love, just spending time together. This is what we do when we get together with our friends. We do the same thing when we get together with God. Prayer takes many forms: mystical prayer, devotional prayer, liturgical prayer, sacred reading, moments of epiphany snatched from our everyday lives. All of it is included in Ignatius's *conversar.*

This is what is meant by the famous Ignatian motto "finding God in all things." "All things" to Ignatius is the whole panoply of human drama—our relationships, our work, our strivings and failures, our hopes and dreams. God can be found in all of it. *Found* does not mean an intellectual exercise of perceiving the presence of the divine. It means engaging God in it, meeting him, dealing with him. It is matter of *conversar*—an intimate conversation and the interacting that takes place between family members who love each other.

Pray with Your Imagination

In the Spiritual Exercises, Ignatius proposes two ways of entering into the Gospels through imaginative prayer. Ignatius's way of praying the Gospels has been so identified with him that the Christian spiritual tradition identifies it as Ignatian contemplation.

Ignatius would never have thought of himself as a highly educated intellectual. He had an advanced degree from the University of Paris, the finest university in Europe at the time. He was well-acquainted with the ideas of leading philosophers and theologians. He was an excellent analytical thinker. But the mental quality of thought that drove his spiritual life was his remarkable imagination. His imagination played a central role in his conversion. Through his many years of directing others he discovered how useful the imagination could be in fostering a deeper relationship with God. Imaginative prayer is recognized as one of the hallmarks of Ignatian spirituality.

Ignatius first grasped the importance of the imagination during his long convalescence from his battle injuries. His key insights about God came through his imagination. The notes he took as he read about the life of Christ filled a 300-page notebook that he treasured for the rest of his life. The lives of the saints inspired him with noble thoughts of what he might do with his life. He told himself "St. Dominic did this, therefore I must do it. St. Francis did this, therefore I must do it." Ignatius then daydreamed about feats of knightly valor and romantic adventures. His idle daydreams alternated between the two.

But these daydreams were not idle at all. His romantic dreams left him restless and discontented. His thoughts of imitating the saints left him cheerful and satisfied. Gradually he understood that spiritual forces lay behind his different feelings. He wrote of himself: "he came to recognize the difference between the two spirits that moved him, the one being from the evil spirit, the other from God." This breakthrough in understanding the source of his feelings is the foundation of the process of Ignatian discernment. It was an insight he reached by using his imagination.

He continued to make liberal use of the imagination and integrated imaginative prayer into the approach to the spiritual life that he outlined in the Spiritual Exercises. In his hands, the imagination becomes a tool to help us know and love God.

Ignatius presents two ways of imagining in the Spiritual Exercises. The first way is demonstrated in a meditation on the mystery of the Incarnation in the second week of the exercises. He asks us to "enter into the vision of God." God is looking down on our turbulent world. We imagine God's concern for the world. We see God intervening by sending Jesus into the maelstrom of life. This type of imagining helps us see things from God's perspective and take on God's qualities of love, compassion, and understanding.

The second method of imagining is to place ourselves fully within a story from the Gospels. We become onlooker-participants and give full rein to our imagination. Jesus is speaking to a blind man at the side of the road. We feel the hot Mediterranean sun beating down. We smell the dust kicked up by the passersby. We feel the itchy clothing we're wearing, the sweat rolling down our brow, a rumble of hunger. We see the desperation in the blind man's face and hear the wail of hope in his words. We note the irritation of the disciples. Above all we watch Jesus—the way he walks, his gestures, the look in his eyes, the expression on his face. We hear him speak the words that are recorded in the Gospel. We go on to imagine other words he might have spoken and other deeds he might have done.

The best-known example of this use of the imagination in the Spiritual Exercises is the contemplation on Jesus' birth in the second week. Ignatius suggests that we imagine "the labors of the journey to Bethlehem, the struggles of finding a shelter, the poverty, the thirst, the hunger, the cold, the insults that meet the arrival of God-with-us." In the course of the Exercises, Ignatius proposes many such scenes from the Gospels for imaginative contemplation. He chooses scenes of Jesus acting rather than Jesus teaching or telling parables. He wants us to see Jesus interacting with others, Jesus making decisions, Jesus moving about, Jesus ministering. He doesn't want us to *think* about Jesus. He wants us to *experience* him. He wants Jesus to fill our senses. He wants us to meet him.

Following Jesus is the business of our lives. To follow him we must know him, and we get to know him through our imagination. Imaginative Ignatian prayer teaches us things about Jesus that we would not learn through scripture study or theological reflection. It allows the person of Christ to penetrate into places that the intellect does not touch. It brings Jesus into our hearts. It engages our feelings. It enflames us with ideals of generous service.

Imaginative prayer makes the Jesus of the Gospels *our* Jesus. It helps us develop a unique and personal relationship with him. We watch Jesus' face. We listen to the way he speaks. We notice how people respond to him. These imaginative details bring us to know Jesus as more than a name or a historical figure in a book. He is a living person. We say what the villagers in John's Gospel told the Samaritan women: "We have come to know him ourselves, and not just from your report."

Knowing the Jesus Who Is Poor

In the Two Standards meditation in the Spiritual Exercises, Ignatius pictures Jesus as poor, powerless, and humble. As we come to know the humility of Jesus, we realize our own human emptiness before the God who desires to fill us with divine life.

Each of the four Gospels is called the Gospel *according to* Matthew, Mark, Luke, or John. They were written under the guidance of the Holy Spirit by human authors who emphasized different aspects of Jesus' character and ministry. They reflect the memories of different Christian communities and they were written to appeal to different audiences. Thus each of them has a distinct flavor.

The same can be said for the picture Ignatius paints of Jesus in the Spiritual Exercises. His imaginative contemplation of the events of the Gospels emphasizes one particular aspect of Jesus' makeup. That is Jesus' poverty. *Poor* is the adjective that Ignatius constantly uses to describe Jesus.

The equivalent noun is *humility*. The Latin root of the word *humility* is *humus*, meaning "earth" or "ground." A humble man is poor, possessing little or nothing of his own. He is a man of the earth.

Ignatius's image of Jesus is the image Paul presents in his letter to the Philippians. Quoting an early Christian hymn, Paul writes of Jesus:

> Though he was in the form of God,
> he did not regard equality with God something to be
>   grasped.
> Rather, he emptied himself,
> taking the form of a slave,
> coming in human likeness;
> and found human in appearance,
> he humbled himself,
> becoming obedient to death,
> even death on a cross. (Philippians 2:6–8)

The Son of God became poor by becoming incarnate. He embraced poverty in the circumstances of his earthly life. God was born in a stable manger and was given the name Jesus. His parents fled with him as refugees to escape a murderous tyrant. Later he lived a simple workman's life in Nazareth. He became an itinerant preacher and teacher, without wife and children, without a home. He died utterly poor—stripped of even his clothing, an executed criminal and outcast, buried in another man's tomb. He had nothing of his own.

For Ignatius, that is the whole point. Jesus clung to nothing. His Father gifted him with abundant gifts and graces. He promptly gave them away to us. Jesus is the exemplar of love. Lovers share whatever they have with the beloved. Jesus shared everything he had with us. He loves us to the very end. Paradoxically, the end is no end at all. Even death is no limit to his love. God raises him up. Jesus shows us that God's love cannot be defeated.

Ignatius invites us to imitate this poor and humble Jesus. He does this in a meditation on the three kinds of humility, one of the pivotal moments in the Spiritual Exercises. The question we are asked to ponder is: What does it mean *for me* to be humble?

The first kind of humility is a desire to be with Jesus to the extent of having no serious rupture with him. We say, "I would want to do nothing that would cut me off from God," Ignatius writes. This is the kind of humility that is necessary for salvation. It is the minimum.

The second kind of humility is a desire to be with Jesus so closely that we strive to eliminate even minor differences between us. "I have come to do your will, O God," was the motive for Jesus' life. That becomes our motive as well. We want above all to seek out and do the will of God.

The third kind of humility is a desire to be so closely identified with Jesus that we experience the suffering and rejection he experienced. We willingly embrace suffering when we have not been at fault. We accept it even when it is no one's fault. Jesus was regarded as an outcast and a fool in his time. We are willing to be seen the same way in our time, "rather than wise or prudent in this world."

Obviously we have more than three choices about how closely we want to identify with Jesus. There is a continuum of humility. Between the minimum and the maximum are many degrees of acceptance of a life being modeled on the life of the poor Jesus. We move along the spectrum in successive stages. Every day we are presented with new opportunities to grow closer to Jesus, or to draw away from him.

Ignatius wants us to know that we have a choice. The meditation on the three kinds of humility reminds us of what the choice is. Jesus had nothing of his own. He has no words except the words that the Father gives him to speak. He does no deeds on his own. He does only what his Father would have him do. He is the one who has been "sent." As he says to Philip, "If you have seen me you have seen the Father."

Perfect humility would have us be able to say the same things about ourselves. We would be poor as Jesus is poor. We have nothing of our own, only what God gives us. We want to speak Jesus' words and do Jesus' deeds. Our whole identity would be summed up in the phrase "son or daughter of God."

Paradoxically, then, we are truly rich, rich with an identity that only God can give and no one can take from us.

Sharing in the Mission of Christ

> Ignatius's choice of scripture passages for contemplating the
> public life of Jesus tend to portray a man-in-action. Jesus is
> on a mission—one who is sent. From the Call of the King
> exercise to the contemplations of the second, third, and
> fourth weeks of the Exercises we realize that Jesus calls us
> to share his mission.

The Jesus who is poor is also the Jesus who is sent. In fact,
the poverty and humility of Jesus lies in his perfect submission to the work that the Father sent him to do. Redeeming
the world involves much work. God is a busy God—active,
ever-present, prodding, suggesting, inviting. He calls us to
share in the work he is doing. This missionary focus is one
of the great themes of Ignatian spirituality.

Let us return to the Call of the King meditation, the
"vision of work" that we looked at briefly in the first chapter.
Ignatius asks us to imagine a great leader who declares his
intention to overcome all the evils that afflict humankind.

The leader asks us to join him. "How could anyone not want to be part of such a noble challenge?" Ignatius asks. This great leader is Jesus himself, who wants everyone to join him in his mission to overcome evil with good everywhere in the world. His call goes out to all peoples, but Ignatius wants each of us to hear it personally.

We note that Jesus takes the initiative. The first followers of Jesus were not restless men looking for a leader. They were fishermen, craftsmen, tax collectors called away from their way of life by a leader who had work for them to do. The same is true for us. Jesus takes the initiative in inviting us to share his mission.

It is a call to each of us personally. In fact to say that Jesus is "calling" us is not quite right. Jesus puts his whole self into it. His voice is strong. His eyes gleam. He reaches out and draws us in. It is better to say that Jesus "beckons" us to join him. Jesus *wants* us to join him. But his beckoning does not contain any element of coercion. God beckons, and then waits for our response. Our human response to God is always free.

The Call of the King is a call to work *with* Christ. When the king says, "whoever wishes to join me in this mission must be willing to labor with me," Ignatius uses the Spanish word *comigo*, meaning "with me." It is an intimate word. We are working alongside Christ. Our being with Christ precedes but includes our working with Christ. In order to be with

Jesus, we find ourselves working alongside him. In other words, our work never takes us away from being with Jesus. This sense of "working with" includes working with others who have also responded to Christ's call. It involves teamwork, working with others. We do not labor alone when we labor with Christ.

The Call of the King requires a response of the heart. Mere intellectual assent is not sufficient. Ignatius describes the "reasonable" response in Ignatius's words: "With God inviting and victory assured, how can anyone in their right mind not surrender to Jesus and his call to labor with him?" Sure, I will do that. There are good reasons to do it; it makes sense.

Ignatius calls for more. "Those who are of great heart and are set on fire with zeal" will throw themselves wholeheartedly into the mission that Jesus has for them. They will say something like this to Christ: "I deeply desire to be with you in accepting all wrongs and all rejections and all poverty, both actual and spiritual—and I deliberately choose this, if it is for your greater service and praise." Obviously we do not make this kind of heart response easily. For most of us it is a goal—the kind of eager, generous offering of ourselves to God that we hope to make someday.

Responding to the Call of the King requires that we think deeply about ourselves. What place does Jesus have in our lives? What has been our relationship with him? What is it now? What do we hope it will become? One way of gauging these questions is to consider the influence Jesus has on our hopes and dreams. Where does he figure in our ambitions? How does he affect our goals? Do we want to serve his purposes in our work? In our interactions with friends and family? Do we want to be an evangelizer? We might be like the rich young man who asked Jesus, "What must I do to inherit eternal life?" Jesus asked him to give up his riches. For this man at least, the challenge was not so much in doing as in letting go. So might it be for many of us.

Ignatius writes that followers of Christ become his instruments. This metaphor grates on many contemporary ears; we bridle at being tools in someone else's hands. But allowing ourselves to become an instrument of God's purposes is a glorious spiritual gift. Ignatius was always begging God to use him. He saw it as a magnificent privilege, as indeed it is. God needs us in a very real sense. Our willingness to be his instruments allows God to act in our created world. It is a role that seems to have lowly status, but it actually elevates us to something like a partnership with God. In doing this we imitate Christ, whose glory was in his perfect submission to his Father's will.

A Way to Clarify Your Values

In the Two Standards meditation, Ignatius helps us see how Jesus comes to emphasize the values he proclaims in the Gospels. If God gifts us with the wealth of our personal gifts, if God gifts us with people's respect, and if God gifts us with a certain self-assurance or pride, why would we value poverty or insults or humility? Ignatius helps us to see how Christ challenges each of us to clarify our values.

What are your values? What standards do you uphold? Are the values you profess the same values that you live by? Ignatius raises the question of values again and again in his Spiritual Exercises. He continually asks us to examine the principles that influence our minds and shape our actions. The values question is complex. We can easily delude ourselves about our values. And it is not enough to simply *profess* values. To truly live our lives as followers of Christ, something more is needed.

The central meditation about values in the Spiritual Exercises is called the Two Standards. In this meditation Ignatius is using the imagery of standards—the battle flags that symbolize the identity of an army. One flag flies in front of the forces of Lucifer, whom Ignatius identifies as "the mortal enemy of our human nature." The other standard flies in front of the camp where Christ is leader. Ignatius would have us enter into this scene imaginatively, to *see* these two leaders in our mind's eye. We are to look at how each leader presents himself—Lucifer on a throne, terrifying amidst smoke and fire, and Christ standing on a lowly place, beautiful and attractive. What kind of instructions does Lucifer issue for waging the battle? How does Christ send forth his followers to win the hearts of others? We are to meditate upon the contrasting values that each leader employs in the struggle for the hearts and minds of human beings.

It is no accident that Ignatius uses the name Lucifer for the commander of the forces of the Lord's enemy. *Lucifer* means "bearer of light." There is an ancient Christian tradition that the devil is a fallen archangel who led a rebellion against God and was expelled from heaven. Another tradition speculates that Lucifer rebelled at the prospect of angels adoring a God-made-man. Ignatius, then, identifies Lucifer not so much as the enemy of God but the "enemy of our human nature." To our human way of thinking, Lucifer's values are not necessarily obviously repugnant and evil.

We need to remember that Lucifer used to be an angel. He bears light, but the ideas, propositions, and values he offers are false lights. They are distortions of the good. We need discernment and a heartfelt understanding to unravel his deceptions.

Lucifer's program for human life is centered on the attractions of riches, honor, and pride. We should not rush to label these "bad" values. Some Christians do this, and indeed some traditions of Christian spirituality are based on a firm rejection of riches, honor, and pride. But the Ignatian perspective is more nuanced. It tells us that nothing in our world is "bad." As Ignatius emphasizes at the beginning of the Spiritual Exercises, "all the things of this world are created because of God's love." Riches, honor, and pride, like everything else in the world, are "presented to us so that we can know God more easily and make a return of love more readily." This is the first complication in clarifying our values.

Those followers identified by the standard of Jesus employ a sharply contrasting strategy. Jesus answers riches, honor, and pride in their deceptive attraction with precisely the opposite values. By his own lived example, Christ offers poverty instead of riches, powerlessness instead of honor, humility in place of pride. Just as Lucifer's values are not obviously "bad," Christ's values are not obviously "good." Poverty, powerlessness, and humility are piously associated with desirable virtue in much of Christian tradition, but these conditions are also afflictions for much of humanity. If we are honest, we must admit that we do not leap to embrace these values. In fact, at face value, they hardly seem values at all.

The Ignatian perspective thus complicates what initially seemed to be a simple picture. Lucifer's program is not simply evil and Christ's program is not obviously good. As good Christian people, we are not now being asked to choose between being a follower of Lucifer or a follower of Christ. Ignatius assumes that we have already made a choice to be allied with Christ in his work in the world. Rather, he wants us to think about the value system that we take on when we do this.

What we need to understand is this: *everything is a gift from God.* This is the fundamental truth of our existence. All created things are "presented to us so that we can know God more easily and make a return of love more readily." The problem with Lucifer's program is that riches, honor, and pride subtly lead us away from this truth. These values delude us about the true nature of things. They focus our attention on ourselves rather than God. We come to think that the wealth we have acquired—whatever we identify as our "riches"—is our accomplishment. The honor we receive is the well-deserved acknowledgment of our importance or our accomplishments. Ultimately, the governing value is pride. We come to believe that we are in charge, that the almighty self takes pride of place.

The values of Jesus lead us back to the fundamental truth. The value of poverty reminds us that we have nothing in ourselves but only as a gift from God. Embracing power-lessness acknowledges that God is our strength. Humility is the expression of the reality of the self before God. It recognizes that we are first and foremost sons and daughters of God, children who call him Father. The perfect embodiment of these values is Jesus himself. The Father exalted the Son because the Son emptied himself in perfect humility by becoming incarnate (a human being). That is why we, in our following of Christ, strive to live by the values of poverty, powerlessness, and humility.

Achieving this understanding about Christ's choice of values is made more difficult by the fact that the Christian values of poverty and powerlessness are honored to some degree in our religious culture. They were not recognized as desirable virtues at all in the ancient world that first heard the gospel, and the fact that most people at least pay lip service to them today is a recognition of how deeply influential Christianity has been. But the familiarity of gospel values can also obscure their radical character.

Ignatius believed that we come to this understanding through God's grace. Explaining is not understanding. The explanation by contrasting Lucifer and Christ here is the barest start on understanding. This, like the other changes that come in the spiritual life, is a matter of the heart. Ignatius would have us beseech God for the grace to understand the strategy of Christ and embrace the values of Christ.

THE GREATEST MARK OF GOD'S LOVE

In the contemplation on the Last Supper which begins
the third week of the Exercises, Ignatius identifies the
Eucharist as "the greatest mark of God's love." For Ignatius
this phrase represents the key to our understanding of our
redemption in Christ.

The reflection on the events of the passion and death of
Jesus in the third week of The Spiritual Exercise begins with
a meditation on the Last Supper and ends with Jesus' burial
in the tomb. The scriptural accounts of these events mostly
portray Jesus as the largely passive victim of the brutal things
other people do to him. But Ignatius uses the word "labor"
often in his instructions for the third week. He sees suffering
and death as Jesus' greatest work. It is what he came to *do*.

The key to understanding this central event of Jesus' life
is contained in two scripture passages that Ignatius wants us
to use as our prayer content as we enter into the third week:
Matthew 26, the Last Supper, and John 13, Jesus washing the

apostles' feet. In suggesting focal points for prayer about these two passages, Ignatius centers on the institution of the Eucharist. In a rare instance of stating his own enthusiastic judgment, Ignatius identifies the moment at the Last Supper when Jesus gave his body and blood for us to eat as the greatest mark of his love.

We often look at Jesus' passion and death as the events that explain the Eucharist. For Ignatius, it is the other way around; the Eucharist explains the meaning of Jesus' passion and death.

The Eucharist tells us that Jesus holds nothing back from us in his love. At the Last Supper, even before his enemies took him, Jesus gave himself to us to be our food. How much does God love us? *That's* how much he loves us. We can consume him. He gives his body and blood to us every day. The Eucharist explains the cross. Through the ages theologians have used many terms to explain the meaning of the passion and death of Christ. They say that Christ has ransomed us with his blood, paid the price to redeem us, satisfied the debt mankind owed, relieved the burden of sin, and so forth. All these images and formulations point toward a truth that the Eucharist proclaims more simply: love costs. It takes a lot to redeem mankind. Jesus is willing to do whatever it takes.

Love costs. On Calvary, love cost Jesus everything. The Eucharist takes this saving act of love out of time and makes it portable. It is everywhere; it is eternally present. Ignatius saw that every Eucharist gives us the opportunity to be swept up into Jesus' act of love for his brothers and sisters. The Eucharist is where Jesus is. It gives purpose and meaning to everything that happens to him. It is the key to his passion and death—an expression of love that is so generous that it sees death as no impediment to God's love.

The Eucharist sums up many themes of Ignatian spirituality. The Ignatian way calls us to be close to Christ and to imitate him. The Eucharist brings us to the most intimate possible relationship with Jesus. The Ignatian way reveals God as a loving God—Love loving. Nothing demonstrates this more clearly than the Eucharist. The Ignatian way is the way of compassion, which unites us with Jesus and our fellow human beings. The Eucharist is the celebration of compassion. The Ignatian way is the way of the heart. The Eucharist shows God to be all heart.

The Eucharist raises one particular Ignatian question in an especially insistent fashion: What is our response to God?

The answer to this question is suggested in John 13, the other scripture passage that Ignatius assigns for the first prayer period of the third week of the Spiritual Exercises. Before Jesus gave the disciples the Eucharist, he washed their feet. This is the work of a servant or slave. Jesus does it and says that this humble service is an example of how we are to act. He demonstrates how we respond to God. We are called to be people who serve. We have received all that we have as a gift from God. We respond to his love by giving it away, by sharing it in our way of serving.

Ignatius may have placed such great emphasis on the Eucharist because of a vision he received not long after his decision to follow Christ. He was attending Mass in the monastery chapel at Manresa in Spain. As he writes in the *Autobiography*, referring to himself in the third person, "at the elevation of the body of Christ Our Lord, he beheld, with the eyes of his soul, white rays descending from above. . . . The manner in which Our Lord Jesus Christ is present in the Blessed Sacrament was clearly and vividly stamped upon his mind." These words are reminiscent of the Contemplation on the Love of God, which ends the Spiritual Exercises. There, we are invited to imagine God's boundless, endless love: "God's love shines down upon me like the light rays from the sun."

This concluding vision recalls the prayer Anima Christi that Ignatius often refers to as part of our closing response to a prayer period. It is a Eucharistic prayer that joins us with Jesus, who continues to give us all that he is. What follows is my own rephrasing of this favorite prayer of Ignatius.

Jesus, may all that is you flow into me.
May your body and blood be my food and drink.

May your passion and death be my strength and life.

Jesus, with you by my side enough has been given.

May the shelter I seek be the shadow of your cross.

Let me not run from the love which you offer,

but hold me safe from the forces of evil.

On each of my dyings shed your light and your love.

Keep calling to me until that day comes,

when, with your saints, I may praise you forever. Amen.

SEEKING THE GRACE OF COMPASSION

In the third week of the Exercises, Ignatius has us consider the gospel events of the passion and death of Jesus. We cannot change what happened. But we can stay with Jesus as he shares his experience with us, and we will be changed.

One of the great challenges of life is the task of bearing pain. We suffer and those whom we love suffer. We instinctively flee from pain, yet it is a fact of life that spiritual, bodily, and emotional suffering is inevitable. In the Ignatian perspective, our graced response to pain is called compassion. The English word *compassion* is drawn from two Latin words meaning "to suffer" and "with." Authentic Christian compassion is a virtue that enables us to share the suffering of others, as well as to bear our own pain. It is a grace, another gifting from God.

Ignatius believed that compassion is the fruit of intimacy with Jesus. Achieving this intimacy is the great theme of Ignatius's Spiritual Exercises. In the first week of the

Exercises we come to terms with our own sin, the deep flaws in our world, and the work that God is doing to remedy the situation. The second week brings us into close contact with Jesus as we meditate on his public ministry and learn what it means to be with him and to work with him. But becoming a true disciple of Jesus means something more: to follow him to the end, to stay with him to his suffering and death.

The third week of the Spiritual Exercises consists of praying over the scriptural accounts of Jesus' passion and death. We feel many emotions as we ponder the suffering and death of Jesus; for example, we might feel pity, horror, gratitude, wonder. But the specific grace that Ignatius would have us seek is the grace of compassion. Ignatius emphasizes how important it is to enter into Jesus' inner experience. We are to *suffer with* Jesus—by our compassion. It is as if Jesus were saying, "Let me tell you what it was like, what I saw, what I felt. Please don't interrupt; just stay with me and listen." The third week ends with us standing compassionately at the tomb of the dead Jesus. There is a sense of emptiness, a void, a darkness. Compassion enables us to stay there in the loneliness.

These contemplations on the passion and death of Jesus teach us about the pain and suffering we encounter in our own lives. First, most of the time, there is nothing we can do about them. Jesus' agony and death are historical facts that cannot be undone. Neither can the circumstances of most of the suffering we experience be substantially altered. People die. Our bodies break down in illness and debility. Relationships crumble. People sin, and sin has lasting consequences. We must accept these facts.

Our third week meditations also teach us how difficult acceptance is. When we cannot change a situation, we are tempted to walk away from it. We might literally walk away; we are too busy to sit with a suffering friend. Or we walk away emotionally; we harden ourselves and maintain an emotional distance. We might react to the Gospel accounts of Jesus' passion and death this way. They describe something terrible and horribly painful, yet we might shield ourselves from the pain. We *know* the story of the Passion. Ignatius wants us to *experience* it as something fresh and immediate. We learn to suffer with Jesus, and thus learn to suffer with the people in our lives.

In the end, we learn that Ignatian compassion is essentially our loving presence. There is nothing we can do. There is little we can say. But we can *be* there.

On the other side of compassion is a sharing in joy. The third week of the Spiritual Exercises is followed by contemplations on Gospel accounts about the risen Jesus in the fourth week. Jesus' pain and suffering are followed by the victorious joy of his resurrection. All seemed lost on Good Friday as we stood by Jesus' tomb, but now the tomb is empty and the risen Jesus lives again. We rejoice because the resurrected Jesus is present to us. We are consoled not because Jesus works miracles and relieves whatever hardship or pain we are now suffering, but because he suffers with us now, just as we have learned to suffer with him.

Compassion also opens us up to God's forgiveness. Ignatius instructs those making the Spiritual Exercises to ask for the grace "to grieve, be sad, and weep" as they contemplate Jesus' sufferings. Compassion of this kind makes us sensitive to the ways that we have failed to love. We have sharpened our sensitivity to God's love, and we are more ready to receive forgiveness.

Earlier in this book we looked at how the Gospel story of Jesus' meal at the house of Simon the Pharisee reveals God's infinite forgiveness. Let us reflect on it again—this time as a story of compassion. A "sinful woman"—a prostitute—comes to Jesus as he reclines at table and bathes his feet with her tears. "Then she wiped them with her hair, kissed them, and anointed them with the ointment."

When Simon and the others at the table are scandalized by this scene, Jesus makes it a teaching moment. He tells a story about a money lender who forgives the debts of two men—one who owed five hundred days' wages, and one who owed fifty days. "Which of them will love him more?" Jesus asks. "The one . . . whose larger debt was forgiven," Simon replies, and Jesus applies the lesson: the sinful woman loved Jesus greatly because she knew that her sins were great. She expresses her love for Jesus not in words but in deeds—deeds that speak. He forgives her sins because "she has shown great love." (Luke 7: 37–47)

Like the sinful woman, we feel safe because we are in Jesus' presence. Compassion enables us to be with him, and so we understand, too, his compassion in being with us. His simple presence provides a continuing consolation for our lives, especially those dark and lonely times when suffering is particularly bitter. His consoling presence in turn allows us to be present to others as Jesus is present to us.

A WAY TO DISCERN GOD'S WILL

One of Ignatius' greatest gifts is his Rules for Discernment which form part of the Spiritual Exercises. He showed how God speaks a language to us through our feelings. Prayer, a growing familiarity with God, and an intimate knowledge of Jesus and his actions are all elements of a discerning heart.

What shall we *do*? We should not do anything wicked and we should not do anything absurd. Between these boundaries lie a vast number of possibilities. We face large decisions: schooling, career, work, state of life, relationships, weighty commitments. Every day we face smaller decisions about our priorities and goals, how to spend our time, what to pay attention to and what to put off for another day. How do we make these choices? How do we weigh competing values? How do we discern the right path?

Ignatian spirituality gives us a way to approach these questions. To follow Jesus we need to know how to make good decisions. Ignatian spirituality helps us approach this challenge in a practical way.

Ignatius would first have us be clear about the ends that we seek. Again we return to the Principle and Foundation for clarity about the values that should govern our choices. Everything in this world is presented to us "so that we can know God more easily and make a return of love more readily." Thus, "our only desire and our one choice should be this: I want and I choose what better leads to God's deepening life in me." Our loving relationship with God is the goal and end of our life. All of our choices are means, steps toward reaching our goal. We enter marriage or choose a career or start a business as a way to deepen our relationship with God. All of these important choices are means, not ends in themselves. It is easy to lose sight of this and treat choices as the ends. Our first choice or decision is simply to be a follower of Christ. Everything else—all our choices, big and small—follows from this.

When we have our end clearly in sight, then we are able to tackle the complexities of decision making. One way is the analytical approach. In trying to choose between two goods, we might list pros and cons in two columns on a sheet of paper. If we are perplexed, we might also ask some friends what they think. Then we make a decision, offer our decision to God for his blessing, and pray for a consolation of peace as God's gift to us.

Ignatius calls this type of decision making a "third-time" choice. "First-time" and "second-time" choices are decisions guided by our hearts, where confirmation comes not from the reasoning intellect but through a discernment of the meaning of the different movements of the emotions and feelings. This is Ignatius's greatest gift to us about decision making. It may be called the gift of the reasoning heart.

A first-time choice is a decision that is unmistakably clear. We *know* what is right. Ignatius cites two examples of first-time choice in the New Testament: the conversion of the apostle Paul, and the call of the tax collector Matthew. Neither man had any doubt about what God wanted of him (at least in these situations). First-time choices are not rare. We probably know people who never had any doubt about what they should do at major turning points in their lives. Some people are sure about their marriage spouse at a first meeting in this graced manner. Others are sure about their religious-life vocation or priestly vocation in a similar way. You may have had this experience yourself, at least in some circumstances.

Second-time choices are situations where the preferred choice is not entirely clear. We are presented with alternative courses of action that all seem attractive to some degree, and we are not blessed with the gift of a clear certainty about what to do. In these cases, Ignatius says that we can discern the right choice by attending to the inner movements of our spirit. In particular, feelings of "consolation" and "desolation" will signal the correct course of action. Ignatius always carefully puts the word *spiritual* before consolation and desolation. For him spiritual consolation is our experience "when some interior movement in the soul is caused, through which the soul comes to be inflamed with love of its Creator and Lord." Ignatius more simply describes consolation as every increase in hope, faith, and charity. Spiritual desolation is just the opposite. The words Ignatius uses to describe it include darkness of soul, disturbance, movement to things low and earthly, disquiet of different agitations and temptations. Ignatius's understanding of the importance of these feelings dates back to the very beginning of his conversion to a fervent Christian faith when he learned to pay close attention to his feelings.

Second-time choice is not simply a matter of "feeling peaceful" about a proposed decision. The feelings of spiritual consolation and spiritual desolation must be carefully assessed. Complacency and smugness about a decision can masquerade as consolation. At times, desolation can be a timely sense of restlessness pointing us in a new direction. Ignatius discusses how to work with his guidelines for discerning at some length in his "rules for discernment of spirits" at the end of the Spiritual Exercises.

It seems surprising (and somewhat risky) to trust our feelings to the degree Ignatius does, but this approach to discernment is entirely consistent with his vision of the Christian life. The Ignatian perspective tells us that we live in a world that is permeated by God, a world God uses to keep in touch with us. We seek to follow Jesus. We carefully observe him in the Gospels and we enter into these Gospel scenes using the methods of Ignatian contemplation through imagination. We come to know who Jesus is and strive to make him the center of our lives. We make our decisions within the context of this relationship of love. It is a relationship of the heart. Our heart will tell us which decisions will bring us closer to Jesus and which will take us away from him.

Ignatian discernment, then, holds that our Christian choices are often beyond the merely rational or reasonable. "The heart has its reasons of which the mind knows nothing," Pascal said. This is fine—as long as the heart has been schooled by Christ.

It is often said that Ignatian spirituality forms us to be "contemplatives in action." We can understand this somewhat paradoxical term if we see that the goal is action and discernment is the means. Discernment guides us to decisions that will join us ever more closely with Christ and with our working with Christ in the world. Contemplation of Jesus in the Gospels is the essential discipline that makes discernment possible. The practice of imaginative prayer teaches us who Jesus is and how he acts and how he decides. This kind of contemplation schools our hearts and guides us to the decisions that bring us closer to God.

WORKING WITH OTHERS

In the Call of the King exercise, Ignatius had emphasized the Spanish word *comigo*, meaning "with me." We work with Christ and also with other people. Even the Ignatian retreat involves the director and the retreatant working together.

Ignatius understood early on that God was calling him to a life of service, but it took him many years to figure out how he was supposed to do this. His first notion was to set off by himself. Solitary individual accomplishment was the knightly ideal of the time, and Ignatius applied this to his new life as a Christian. He conceived of himself as a Christian knight in service of his Lord. This did not work out very well. As a solitary pilgrim, he went to the Holy Land, but was forced to return home. He began to teach others about the spiritual life, but ran afoul of mistrustful inquisitors, who were deeply suspicious of lone itinerant preachers sharing their spiritual insights with others.

The real change in Ignatius's style of ministry came when he went to the University of Paris to get the education he needed to teach about the faith. He notes what happened in a brief comment in his autobiography. He studied philosophy and theology, he writes, "and gathered about him a number of companions." These companions were the men who became the first members of the Society of Jesus. From this point on Ignatius always worked in concert with others. The Jesuit order has included many outstanding individuals with exceptional skills and talents, but Jesuit ministry, and the ministry of others formed in Ignatian spirituality, has always been formulated in a spirit of collaboration.

Collaboration is built into the very structure of the Spiritual Exercises. Ignatius intended that the Exercises be undertaken not alone but with the help of a spiritual director. The term *director* is actually something of a misnomer. "The director's role is that of being a helper to us in retreat," Ignatius writes at the beginning of the Exercises. This person does not "direct" but rather guides and helps. The relationship between God and the retreatant is always the focus of the Exercises, but we do not examine this relationship alone. We are to do it collaboratively, with the assistance of a wise and trusted guide who can help us be sensitive to the Spirit's movements and arrive at a discerning interpretation of these movements for our spiritual growth.

Much of the spiritual director's work involves careful listening to the retreatant's account of what happens in prayer and during the retreat. The director helps us filter out what is extraneous and focus on the essential. With help, we are able to see how apparently scattered things come together in a meaningful pattern. The director helps us learn the "language of God" spoken through the various media that flood our lives. With the help of our spiritual director we come to understand that our relationship with God is a real relationship with ups and downs, a give and take.

It is a relationship in which the parties collaborate on a mission of service to others. We have seen how the meditation the Call of the King presents Jesus' call to work with him. Jesus' call to join him in his work in the world means that we are to serve with others as well as with Christ. Paul uses the striking metaphor of the body to express the interrelatedness of those who respond to Jesus' call to join him in his mission. We are all parts of the body of Christ, he writes. He continues:

> God placed the parts, each one of them, in the body as he intended. If they were all one part, where would the body be? But as it is, there are many parts, yet one body. The eye cannot say to the hand, "I do not need you," nor again the head to the feet, "I do not need you." . . . God has so constructed the body . . . that there may be no division in the body, but that the parts may have the same concern for one another. If (one) part suffers, all the parts suffer with it; if one part is honored, all the parts share its joy. (1 Corinthians 12:18–21,24,25–26)

Christian ministry and mission can never be seen as an individualistic enterprise. We always interact as members of the body of Christ. We always serve in the context of a relationship with Christ and with others. One of the great gifts we share with others is the fruit of these life-giving relationships. Ministry is a sharing of life and love. Jesus gives us the gift of divine life, and invites us to join him in giving this life to others. Ministry in the Ignatian mode is based on Jesus' promise that "where two or three are gathered together in my name, there am I in the midst of them." (Matthew 18:20)

Service in the Ignatian way can be summarized as a progression through the interlocking elements of Ignatian spirituality that we have been discussing. We might describe them in an ever continuing flow from beginning to end and back to the beginning in this way:

Jesus. He is the center of our lives. The One who leads. The One who calls us to serve others.

Vision. We try to grasp the big picture: the reign of God is breaking into our world.

Exercising. We do things—not for others but with them. We do them with Jesus.

Reflecting. We observe where God is at work and where he is absent.

Valuing. We clarify the values present in a situation and ask Jesus to shape them.

Choosing. We reflect on the possible courses of
action and choose what seems better.

Discerning. We listen to the language of our hearts.

More. We strive to do the better thing out of love for
God.

Laboring. We collaborate with Christ in the work of
redeeming and healing the world.

Thanking. All is gift. Thanksgiving permeates our
lives.

BEING HELPFUL

Ignatius emphasizes one Spanish word throughout the Exercises: *ayudar*, meaning " to help." This word also becomes the simplest way for him to describe any ministry that we do. "To help" is a humble way of serving.

In 1537, an anxious Ignatius Loyola was on the road to Rome with his companions. He was confused and discouraged about service. He and his companions, the first Jesuits, had vowed to serve the Lord together, but they didn't have a clear idea of what they should be doing. They initially thought that they should go to the Holy Land, but these plans had been thwarted. Now they were pursuing plan B—a plan to go to Rome to put themselves at the disposal of the pope.

Ignatius stopped at a roadside chapel in the little town of La Storta a few miles outside Rome and prayed about the problem. He implored Mary to give him the assurance that he would be with her Son. For some time now his prayer had been "place me with your Son." Ignatius was then blessed with an extraordinary mystical vision. He saw God the Father, and he saw Jesus carrying his cross. The Father says to Ignatius: "we will be propitious [favorably disposed] to you in Rome." Then the Father tells Jesus, "I want you to take this man to serve us." Then Jesus says to Ignatius, "We want you to serve us."

Ignatius went on to Rome, and the Society of Jesus was indeed blessed by many graces, something that Ignatius saw as a fulfillment of the La Storta vision. Jesuit tradition has seen this vision as a promise of divinely blessed mission to the whole Society of Jesus. Today we understand this vision as applying to everyone who is influenced by Ignatian spirituality. The vision shows our mission as God's work, not ours. We serve as partners with Jesus in *his* work. We do not set out on our own. La Storta describes an active vision of service. The risen Jesus is not *on* the cross; he is *carrying* the cross. He is going somewhere. Finally, the cross is central to this vision of our accompaniment. This is the ultimate symbol of divine love poured out for us. Our own service is love poured out, sometimes in a crucifying way for us.

Ignatius used several metaphors to describe the nature of our service to God. Military imagery is prominent in the Spiritual Exercises. The meditation on the Call of the King invites us to personally commit ourselves to join the resurrected Christ in the continuing struggle to achieve the kingdom of God. The meditation called the Two Standards imagines two armies clashing—one under the banner of Lucifer, one under the standard of Christ. However, when he wrote the Constitutions of the Society of Jesus, Ignatius chose a different image of service—the scriptural image of the laborers in the vineyard from Matthew 20:

> The kingdom of heaven is like a landowner who went out at dawn to hire laborers for his vineyard. After agreeing with them for the usual daily wage, he sent them into his vineyard. Going out about nine o'clock, he saw others standing idle in the marketplace, and he said to them, "You too go into my vineyard, and I will give you what is just." So they went off. (And) he went out again around noon, and around three o'clock, and did likewise. Going out about five o'clock, he found others standing around, and said to them, "Why do you stand here idle all day?" They answered, "Because no one has hired us." He said to them, "You too go into my vineyard." (Matthew 20:1–7)

The vineyard is the symbol of God's world. It is a busy place, full of life and activity and growth, and God seeks out people to tend it—to plant and cultivate and harvest. He calls to everyone throughout the day—young and old, rich and poor, men and women in all conditions of life. There is something for all of us to do, and the wages for all of us are the same, whether we labor long or briefly—intimacy with Jesus and fulfillment of our life's purpose.

The words *mission* and *ministry* have a lofty connotation. Ignatius described service much more simply. He used the

Spanish word *ayudar*—"to help." The work of the Jesuits, he often said, was to "help souls." Ignatian spirituality manifests a profound respect for the work that God is doing in the lives of others. We help others respond to God's invitation. We work *with* Jesus.

Everyone can help. Helping does not require extensive training and a fistful of academic degrees. Very young people can help; so can the very old. We do not need a ministry to serve in the Ignatian sense. We can be helpful in the ordinary course of our day-to-day lives—at work, at home, in our families and neighborhoods, in our relationships with loved ones and passing acquaintances.

Many things "help." Jesuits work in an astonishing variety of activities—not only education and pastoral work, but also communications, law, the arts and sciences, medicine, and virtually all professions. Ignatian spirituality opens a vast landscape of service. We can serve God in many ways as long as we understand service as essentially sharing with others the life that God has given us.

In helping others, we need to be wise, discerning, and disciplined. We do not have to be anxious about helping souls. We can relax because we are working alongside God. God calls us to service and he gives us colleagues and friends to work with. The work is his. We are merely helping him with it.

Jesus Is All Heart

Ignatius does not use the word *heart* in his text of the Exercises. But the kind of response that he seeks in the retreat can best be summed up in the imagery of a heart-felt response.

Intimacy with Jesus is the central grace of the Spiritual Exercises. The journey begins in the first week as we confront the damage done by sin and learn of God's plan to repair it. In the second week Christ invites us to work alongside him in his work to redeem the world. The third week brings us face to face with Jesus' continuing presence in the world, especially in the Eucharist, "the greatest mark of his love." Finally, in the fourth and concluding week, we experience the risen Jesus who rejoices to share with us the boundless intimacy of his resurrected life.

The concluding Contemplation on the Love of God has us reflect on the limitless blessings of God that cascade down on our world like the rays of the sun. Our response is the great Suscipe prayer:

> Take, Lord, and receive all my liberty, my memory, my
> understanding, and my entire will—all that I have and call
> my own. You have given it all to me. To you, Lord, I return
> it. Everything is yours; do with it what you will. Give me
> only your love and your grace. That is enough for me.

Intimacy holds nothing back. The partners to a truly intimate relationship share everything. This is the place to which Ignatius brings us—a place where we share everything we have with Jesus our beloved, as he shares everything with us.

Throughout the centuries, the traditional image for total commitment has been the image of the heart. Jesus' heart is in it. He holds nothing back from us. His heart is set on having an intimate relationship with us. The core theme of Ignatian spirituality is *Jesus is all heart*.

Jesus is all heart. This is what Ignatius saw in the vision at La Storta, when he was on his way to Rome to place the Society of Jesus at the service of the pope. While praying in the chapel, Jesus appeared to him carrying his cross and said, "we want you to serve us." Jesus was carrying his cross, giving everything he has. He was inviting Ignatius (and all of us) to join him in his ongoing work of healing and redemption.

Jesus is all heart. In the seventeenth century, Jesus appeared to the French nun Margaret Mary Alacoque and asked her to spread the news of his love and mercy throughout the world. The image she saw was that of the Sacred Heart. Jesus' physical heart was the emblem of his divine love. From it flowed all the promises of Jesus' love, including peace in families, consolation in times of trouble, and mercy for sinners. The great promoter of devotion to the Sacred Heart was a Jesuit, Fr. Claude la Colombiere, Margaret Mary Alacoque's spiritual director.

Ignatius included no novenas, offices, or other devotional practices in the Spiritual Exercises. Jesuits have not been associated with traditional devotions as have other religious orders. The Sacred Heart is a partial exception. Beginning with Fr. la Colombiere, Jesuits have been among the most active promoters of devotion to the Sacred Heart. This is no surprise, because heart-of-Christ devotion is truly integral to Ignatian spirituality. It focuses our attention on the hold-nothing-back love that Jesus has for us. It directs us to the nature of our response to this love—a response of the heart, a whole person response, a response that holds nothing back. The heart of Christ symbolizes his love—the most important symbol representing Christ. The heart stands for all of Christ. Jesus is all heart.

In the concluding chapter of his Gospel, the apostle John describes Jesus' farewell to his disciples on the shore of the Sea of Galilee. Jesus cooks breakfast for his friends and then takes Peter aside for a little chat. Three times Jesus asks Peter, "do you love me?" Three times Peter insists that he loves Jesus fervently. He is distressed that Jesus asks the question more then once. "You *know* that I love you," he insists. But Peter's love hasn't always been so evident. It is clear that Jesus prods Peter to declare his love three times in order to reverse Peter's three denials of Christ not long before, when Peter was terrified that Jesus' enemies would arrest him too.

On the shores of the lake, Peter understands that he has been forgiven. Not only that—he has been given work to do. Three times, in response to Peter's three declarations of love, Jesus says "feed my lambs." He is teaching Peter an important lesson. Peter's mission is to serve others, and the gifts he gives to others are the gifts he has received. Peter cannot change the past. But he has been forgiven for the wrongs he has done. He has been bathed in the grace of the loving heart of God. That loving heart is the gift Peter gives to those he serves. It is our gift too.

In John's Gospel, Jesus' last words to Peter—and to us—are "follow me." He invites us to be *with* him. Elsewhere Jesus asks us to "take my yoke upon you." A yoke is a wooden apparatus that binds two animals so they can pull together. Jesus was a carpenter and he knew about yokes. He probably made yokes for the customers of the Joseph and Son carpentry business in Nazareth. It is a vivid image. Jesus' yoke connects us intimately with him. It allows us to labor together. Through it we sense Jesus' direction and feel Jesus' power.

That yoke is love. It is our generous response to the limitless love that God pours onto his creation. It draws us into the intimate relationship of Christ that satisfies our deepest desires and fulfills our grandest dreams, the dreams that our loving God has for us.

FURTHER READING

Works by St. Ignatius Loyola

Draw Me Into Your Friendship: A Literal Translation and a Contemporary Reading of the Spiritual Exercises. David L. Fleming, SJ. St. Louis: Institute of Jesuit Sources.

A Pilgrim's Testament: The Memoirs of Saint Ignatius of Loyola. Translated by Parmananda R. Divarkar. St. Louis: Institute of Jesuit Sources.

Constitutions of the Society of Jesus & Their Complementary Norms. St. Louis: Institute of Jesuit Sources.

Books on Ignatian Spirituality

Inner Compass: An Invitation to Ignatian Spirituality. Margaret Silf. Chicago: Loyola Press.

Ignatian Humanism: A Dynamic Spirituality for the 21st Century. Ronald Modras. Chicago: Loyola Press.

A Friendship Like No Other. William A. Barry, SJ. Chicago: Loyola Press.

The Ignatian Workout: Daily Spiritual Exercises for a Healthy Faith. Tim Muldoon. Chicago: Loyola Press.

ABOUT THE AUTHOR

David L. Fleming, SJ, is editor of the journal *Review for Religious* and the author of many books on Ignatian spirituality and spiritual direction, including *Like the Lightning*, *Prisms for a Christ-Life*, and *Draw Me into Your Friendship*. He holds a doctorate in spiritual theology from the Catholic University of America.

Loyola Press—helping you find God in all things

LOYOLA PRESS.

A JESUIT MINISTRY

(800) 621-1008

For more information on Ignatian resources, please visit www.loyolapress.com

Other Ignatian Titles from Loyola Press

A Friendship Like No Other:
Experiencing God's Amazing Embrace
William A. Barry, SJ • 2702-8 • $14.95

Ignatian Humanism:
A Dynamic Spirituality for the 21st Century
Ronald Modras • 1986-3 • $16.95

An Ignatian Spirituality Reader
George W. Traub, SJ • 2723-3 • $18.95

The Ignatian Workout:
Daily Spiritual Exercises for a Healthy Faith
Tim Muldoon • 1979-5 • $14.95

Inner Compass:
An Invitation to Ignatian Spirituality
Margaret Silf • 2645-8 • $14.95

A Jesuit Education Reader
George W. Traub, SJ • 2722-6 • $24.95

Making Choices in Christ:
The Foundations of Ignatian Spirituality
Joseph A. Tetlow, SJ • 2716-5 • $12.95

Stretched for Greater Glory:
What to Expect from the Spiritual Exercises
George A. Aschenbrenner, SJ • 2087-6 • $17.95

Available at your local bookstore, or visit www.loyolapress.com
or call 800-621-1008 to order.